The Dance at St. Gabriel's

poems by Felix Stefanile

The Dance at St. Gabriel's

Story Line Press & Peterloo Poets

1995

Story Line Press; Three Oaks Farm; Brownsville, OR 97327

Peterloo Poets; 2 Kelly Gardens; Calstock, Cornwall PL18 9SA U. K.

This publication was made possible thanks in part to the generous support of the Nicholas Roerich Museum, the Andrew W. Mellon Foundation, the National Endowment for the Arts, and our individual contributors.

Book design by Chiquita Babb

Library of Congress Cataloging-in-Publication Data

Stefanile, Felix, 1920–
    The Dance at St. Gabriel's : poems / by Felix Stefanile.
        p. cm.
    ISBN 1-885266-08-1
    1. Italian Americans—Poetry.   I. Title.
PS3569. T339D36   1995
811'.54—dc20   95-6896
                                                      CIP

Acknowledgments

Some of the poems in this book were originally published in magazines, and elsewhere. I note the publications that follow with gratitude: *Canto, The Centennial Review, Elizabeth, Footwork: The Paterson Literary Review; Kayak, La Fusta, The Lyric, Modern Age, New Letters, The New York Times, Occident, Poetry* (Chicago), *Poetry Broadside, Poetry Now, River City Review, Saturday Review, The Sewanee Review, The Sycamore Review, Yankee.*

    The two translations from the Italian of Umberto Saba were originally published in *Umberto Saba: 31 poems,* issued by the Elizabeth Press in 1978 with the permission of Linuccia Saba, ("Ulysses," and "The Boy and the Shrike"). "The Dance at St. Gabriel's," title poem, was originally published in *From the Margin: Writings in Italian Americana,* published by the Purdue University Press in 1991. "Driving East, Thinking of Frank O'Hara" was originally published in *Voyages to the Inland Sea, VIII,* University of Wisconsin-LaCrosse.

Contents

When we journey into life it is in the company of a good angel, who has been bestowed on us in the guise of a close companion. Even those of us who do not sense the good luck this companion brings will nevertheless feel a deep loss the moment the border is crossed from our country, when the angel forsakes us.

The Brothers Grimm
adapted from a translation by Robert Ward

These poems are for Selma.

I.

The Dance at St. Gabriel's

I am a child of the Depression,
and no one can take that away from me.

Marion K. Stocking

On Theory and Practice

To make the familiar strange, that is a touch
that can anoint, that can transform the self.
Make the strange familiar, agitate
the consciousness. Then everything you feel
is revelation. What is tame is shame,
the absence of a probing mind. Forget
all talk of contours, and accomplishment
of right surprise will lurk at every hand.

How hard he tried, Van Gogh, in, out of touch
with his familiar lump of world and self:
his daubs and scrapes and scratches agitate
the consciousness. Old Shoes. And yet you feel
the world's accessibility as no shame,
though acceptance is a doze. Forget
the laziness of fact. Accomplishment
is the old brush that trembles in Van Gogh's hand.

Grandfather's Story

My mother bathed me in warm wine
for I was weak and puny at my birth.
The wine kept me alive, and I grew stronger.
My father warmed the wine
with a horseshoe burned red hot.
Thus I took in the cleverness of wine,
the endurance of iron.
To cool me then my mother cradled me
in the new leaves
of a blooming chestnut tree.
Soft, soft was the touch,
and I slept mightily.

The Light-Bringer

A little kitchen: in the window's gloom
the coal-stove goes on purring like a cat
with one lid slitted open, crescent eye
casting its livid wink into the hall.
My father enters, holding in his hand
a mantle, as we called it in those days,
a small hood of wire-mesh to snug around
the gas-jet on the wall. I'm there somehow,
staring with all my might. He slides a chair
against the wall, climbs up, and does his trick
of pulling out a match and striking it
against his pants leg. It hisses, spurts alive.
I understand my part. I clank the stove-lid
back into its flange. Everything turns dark
except for match-light, and the tiny star
that twinkles in my father's eye. But I
know what will happen next. The mantle glows,
and as he turns the jet the flame grows full,
the kitchen blooms with light, darkness dispelled.
Then he hops down, whizzing the chair towards me
with a sudden grin. The window pane is gleaming.

Hanging Out

Standing on corners, waiting for the girls,
smiles on our faces, holes in our shoes,
we whistled and the sparrows whistled back.
The moonlight lay like cracked glass at our feet.

Standing on corners, waiting for the girls,
our blood did all our thinking for us then.
Beans for brains, as poor as pigeons,
who was it that worked steady in those days,

standing on corners, waiting for the girls?
The wind, like a cop barking, kept us in line.
We stepped between the puddles as we walked.
What happened to the girls? The girls ran home.

The Catch

Your college learn you be smart, talk fancy. You go with the girls, talk fancy. You tell your mother, Ma, why you got the bun on your head, old fashion. Your college learn you don't respect your mother. Some college. Now you say this girl you live together, marriage never mind, old fashion. Your mother cry, and with the beads pray pray and pray. What you think, she ask me. You know what I think, boy? I think if you was pig we raise by and by we sell you for money now, not your mother cry.

The Americanization of the Immigrant

Your words, Genoveffa,
through the open window,
telling me once again
what to buy at the store—
don't forget, don't forget—
aroma of fresh bread
almost a halo.

That was a long time ago.
I never forgot.
Like Dante
I have pondered and pondered
the speech I was born to,
lost now, mother gone,
the whole neighborhood bull-dozed,
and no one to say it on the TV,
that words are dreams.

December, 1941

Pearl Harbor week: the campus in a frenzy,
and the Dean calling chapel every day
so we could listen to the dignitaries
entrained from Washington, or Fort Somewhere.
Loudspeakers sprouted from each corner lamp-post,
reminding us of Hitler's Germany;
recruiting booths sprang up in all the squares,
and the Marines stood guard by Lincoln's bust.

In Latin class but five of us showed up
to meet with Halliday, grumpy as usual.
The bell rang, and he started to call roll
when Melton entered, walking on tip-toe,
a wide grin on his chubby face. He clattered
getting to his seat, and Halliday
stared at him, thanked him for his kind attention.

Melton burst out, "I'm switching. I've just been . . . "
He babbled on about V-8, V-12,
and other officer enlistment programs
now opening up, with schooling guaranteed,
and then a little hitch in the Reserve
if war was over when he finished training.
He seemed to need confirming, kept it up,
"I'm going to dental school; it's a good break,
I'll wind up a commissioned officer."
What this amounted to was a three year deferment.

Old Halliday let loose his glare and grunted,
"I'm happy you're so ready to do duty."
Our small group stiffened. Melton was an ass,
and Halliday no help. No wisdom there
that nasty, frigid, gravel-colored day.
We looked down at our books, and shuffled papers.

Years later, in a tavern—it was peace time,
though U. S. troops were fighting in Korea—
I bumped into Don Mills, a fresh M. A.,
just out of college through the GI Bill.
Immediately he told me about Melton;
he was in South Korea, pulling teeth.
We grinned and grinned, and bought each other drinks.

The Dance at St. Gabriel's

for Louis Otto

We were the smart kids of the neighborhood
where, after high school, no one went to school,
you NYU and I CCNY.
We eyed each other at St. Gabriel's
on Friday nights, and eyed each other's girls.
You were the cute, proverbial good catch
—just think of it, nineteen—and so was I,
but all we had was moonlight on our minds.
This made us cagey; we would meet outside
to figure how to dump our dates, go cruising.
In those hag-ridden and race-conscious times
we wanted to be known as anti-fascists,
and thus get over our Italian names.
When the war came, you volunteered, while I
backed in by not applying for deferment,
for which my loving family named me Fool.
Once, furloughs overlapping, we met up,
the Flight Lieutenant and the PFC;
we joked about the pair we made, and sauntered.
That Father Murray took one look at us,
and said our Air Force wings were the only wings
we'd ever earn. We lofted up our beers.
Ah, Louis, what good times we two have missed.
Your first time up and out the Germans had you,
and for your golden wings they blew you down.

Soldiers and Their Girls

(First Three-Day Pass)

Those years before Fast Food a pizza meant
a neighborhood, an accent maybe, or
the way the customers looked. You had your limits.
One train-stop more it might be Fish and Chips

or Blintzes. What a way to spend a date,
skipping from joint to joint, and getting drunk
on laughter and strange sipping, stupid jokes
about the squid, rose-water, or flat bread.

Whatever, down it went. You smiled and smiled
because the girl was pretty and was proud
and scared. She wanted you to know
Armenians were just like you, or Jews,

and we were all Americans anyway.
You checked your watch, said "Hitler!" She teared up,
pert Rosie Ohanessian, whose large eyes
were darker than that last night on your mind.

She walked you to the depot. You held hands,
but never made a move, the station crammed,
young couples slouching, grinning, waiting for
the speaker to announce the bus from camp.

Edie

Rockingham, N. H.

A night in May, the Bull was on a spree
up in the sky, the Germans had surrendered,
and Edie Johnson was so good to me.
We talked about Japan, and a long war,

and this made Edie very, very tender.
"Don't just sit there!" she laughed, and pulled me forward.
The radio was singing sweet surrender
as we two clasped and struggled without let.

Ah, Edie, I was new at it, and scared,
but I advanced, your puppy on all fours,
and headlong through that night, though trumpets blared,
we only heard ourselves, the little whispers.

We never met again. Wouldn't you know
our orders were being cut that very dawn
when I, dog-tired, snoring in my bunk,
heard the damn whistle, then the hullabaloo

of sergeants, scuttlebutt, and duffle-bags
dragged across bare wooden floors, the thunk
of army trucks pulled up right to the doors,
and the gates slamming. I had no time to think,

and by the telephone MPs kept the score.
My number never came. Now years between

the health and heartache of so many wars
I wonder what I might have said

if I had gotten through. Dear mentor, cunning one,
your page-boy all messed up, your patience of a saint,
your body like a fragrant loaf of bread,
why do you still gleam, the laser in my head?

I sometimes hope you only think I died
in the Pacific, your consoling dream,
and that you talk about me, bleary-eyed,
at The Finn's Place, outside of Rockingham,
where you still go, where Memory belongs—
but that stuff only happens in old songs.

Ballad of the War Bride

Willie, on leave, got married, and came home
to show his discharge, and show off his bride,
a gangling, giggling girl from Birmingham
without a cent. His mother almost died.

His father came right out and talked expense,
and told them that this wasn't Alabam.
The kids agreed. As if doing penance
they both found jobs, and soon the money came.

His mother grumbled on, as did his father;
they said they couldn't understand her speech.
A girl with yellow hair was too much bother,
and they were sure that she was using bleach.

One day they told him, fever in their eyes,
"Kick in more money, and we'll save for you."
Then it was that Willie, past surprise,
knew what he and his sweetheart had to do.

One morning, trim deportment a pure sham,
they left for work as far as one could tell,
but with train tickets back to Birmingham.
He called his folks en route, and told them to go to hell.

L'Ultima Rinunzia

One to suffer, one to cause suffering.
Guido Gozzano

My mother wept, her sickness sure;
solace I had none at heart.
For a poem I kept trying,
while my mother lay there dying.
"Son," she called, "leave your art;
bring me water for my cure."

"I shall call the girl," I said,
"for my work is much too dear.
You may talk to her, and pray
until the coming of the day,
but I must be busy here.
Music fills my head."

Then my mother ceased her turning.
With the coming of the dawn
all my verses seemed to dance.
Sun flashed, like a lance,
shearing steeple, roof, and stone,
toward my window burning, burning.

Ballade of the Sad Celebrities

There goes Jane Fonda with her heavy load
of money. She is shimmering up and down
like mountain laurel rippling by the road
in a bright rush of wind. I like her gown,
and the prim face she wears to bear her crown
of cares, ideals, and other cosmic fears.
A ton of money's not a lot of fun;
winners, when they wince, are winsome dears.

And here comes Johnny, bouncy as a toad
across my TV screen. Such is renown
he scarcely needs a surname. He's the goad
to spur me on to bed where I can drown
my tears of envy for all that I don't own.
His quips and quarrels, and his little leers,
come off as boyishness, the cute put-on;
winners, when they wince, are winsome dears.

But I must prate no more, not incommode;
I am no tenor, crying like a clown
all the way to the bank. If this is code
it's paradox, which is no common noun,
but a high dresser, always on the town.
Fame is performing, fears and leers and tears,
and showmanship's the thing, the lovely one:
winners, when they wince, are winsome dears.

Dear Jane, dear Johnny, I am still alone;
you try your best, but you are not my peers,
though I wish, like you, I could finesse a frown.
Winners, when they wince, are winsome dears.

Rewriting the Cagney and Lacey Show

Tyne Daly, how I love you! Where'd you get
that broad Queens accent, and those flaring eyes?
Your quiet smile, it puts me in a fret;
are you my cousin Josie in disguise?

Of all the hard-boiled girls, and pretty too,
that ever rode Bus 68 at five—
there goes another day—tell me, are you
the one whose stupid brother gave her jive

about becoming an old maid, the one
who wanted his shirt ironed every time
you sat down to do your nails? Did we have fun
once, at some wedding, dancing on a dime?

What a fine topic, Tyne, you are, my theme,
my blooming, bumptious, sharp-tongued TV ghost.
You summon up my past, the streets of Queens,
and Time, the unexpected, welcome guest.

You bring the fantasies, not my cold beer:
the law and order thing, and love on show,
the family, the husband, children near,
and your cop-friend, another woman too.

I bask in the cheap moonlight of the screen,
remembering the girl I never met,

the one who's missing from your cozy scene,
gun put away, and mama baking bread.

I think how nice the world was meant to be
a hundred years ago, on Northern Boulevard.
Her name was Carmen, and she looked at me
across the girls' fence in the old school-yard.

A small boy running past me tossed a note,
a crumpled wad that, opened, simply read,
"Meet me, 3:30. I have a red coat."
It frightened me, I felt my ears turn red,

but I waited all the same, at my "appointed hour."
How could I know that very afternoon
she would turn sick? Sent home, she found no cure.
Next morning teacher told us she was gone.

Those were the years the sexes played apart.
I barely knew her name, or gave a look.
That's how it went, the fright, the shock, the start.
Time has a thing to give me I still lack.

Ah, Tyne, some nights I'm more than just a fan.
Then I become the ghost, not you, the gust
that riffles in your hair, some bathrobe scene
perhaps, with you and Harvey, nothing lost

of that eye-speech cameras carry well
in all those lights and shadows. I'm the script
you're playing to, us millions of jokers all,
your vast, synaptic web, your velvet crypt

of stitched, unstitched electrons on a grid
that is your galaxy. We blink, and you blink back.
It is the night we read, soft, closed eye-lid
of space, on which the capillaries track

their filaments of color, densities
of darkness; blood throbs; buttons flash.
My head's my video, and what it sees
is Carmen, Tyne, but never simple flesh.

What is the relevance of all this jazz?
There's me, in an old house, in a small town
in the midwest; there's you, dear apparition
on a glass, and there's the arty razzmatazz

of music, dialogue, the counterpoint
of staging interspersed with local ads
in other dramas, a collage of cant.
I'm giddy, but I am not driven mad.

I'm driven back into myself, where you
appear, erect and still, like Memory,

the mothering muse whose stories are all true,
the happy ending like the god's decree.

Another house, another town, the viewer
is fooling with the dial, catches your face
and settles back, and smiles. This much is sure:
the stuff of legends is gathering apace.

In the back-yards dogs whimper, garage-doors
give back the light of stars, the glow of lamps.
This is the peace that memory restores,
a splintered moon that glints in hollow stumps
where water settled when the rains came down.
It's water deep enough for dreams to drown,
and in the house the TV roars and roars.

Some Mentors

1. To Answer Robert Frost

(for Spencer Brown)

The question that he frames in all but words
is what to make of a diminished thing.

Some things are best unsaid, and best unheard;
not every tattle-tale's a pretty bird,
but here's one now, that cardinal again.
He must proclaim himself. There are no flowers,
the land is bare, but he makes up for ten,
say cardinal flowers from the summer past.
The weather's threatening; we've had snow-showers,
and biting wind in heavy overcast.
The radio keeps bragging about the fall
in temperature; he won't shut up at all.
He may be saying this is for the birds,
and he's an omen. Furies liked to sing.
He may be telling us in his own words,
"If Rage is all that's left, Rage is a pleasant thing."

2. Cheering Amy Lowell On: "Some Imagist Poems, 1915"

An editor once put her picture in
the paper. Read the caption: because she
was a grand lady, and by no means thin,
he wrote down, "Amy Lowell and Company."
That brought some laughs and chuckles. As for me,
I still remember being called "Cross-Eyes"
when I was small. Grew out of that, grew wise;
I'm on the lookout now for courtesy.

Lord save us from the likes of Ezra Pound
who made a nasty pun out of her name
because of a book. A matter of some fame,
she faced him down, and took part of his ground,
because, though lacking graces, she had grit,
and like her money, used it, used it, used it.

3. *Taking Sides with John Ciardi*

—some words on minus-American poetry

When Robert Lowell hyphenated you—
Italian, hyphen sign, American—
to praise your poetry, your answer ran
in rough-house expletives. Your passion flew,
and subsequently in an interview
you squelched his harmless seeming little hyphen
as not the way to write out citizen.
How culture-vultures smiled at the to-do.

If this is poetry, as may be true,
it's also punctuation, not too thin
a point or line for morals that you drew.
We all know grammar can stick like a pin,
and those who think my point is overdrawn,
they are no friends of yours, nor of mine, John.

Driving East, Thinking of Frank O'Hara

You don't refuse to breathe do you
Frank O'Hara

You're gone now
from the chummy New York you got used to,
Frank—
you don't know the Museum of Modern Art
is still going begging,
the city is broke,
the parks are being abandoned to the Vandals.
Where did you pick up your lingo, so frou-frou,
so in,
like the palaver a lover might send
in a night letter,
full of outrageous code words?
They're mostly chat, your poems,
it is that simple,
and maybe the strap-hanger humming to himself
in the subway under the river
is what they make up,
the fantasies of a reasonable optimist
on a clammy Friday night,
the end of a busy week.

They're not that simple.
They remind me of Jackson Pollock,
whom I don't care for
as I care for you.
I always wish that Pollock had painted words
to accompany his long arm drips and scrawls

with a handy caption.
We know why you liked him so much:
you wrote the way he painted.
The pavements were your canvas
wherever you strolled tee hee and tsk tsk
gaping at windows,
or glimpsing a headline,
or waving to some pretty someone you didn't know on a bus.

They aren't poems, your poems,
they simply breathe
the way you breathed
the dust and oil-slick of the Queen of Cities,
knowing you had to breathe, or else keep still
for a very long time.
They are poems that take a walk—
though not like Prufrock, more like Apollinaire—
as you talk to yourself and your friends,
humming humming and humming
between the snatches of conversation,
and letting the words spill richly, just like paint,
all over your cozy dominion
of street and lobby, luncheonette and bookstore.

You are my favorite action-painter, Frank:
I can always follow the gist of your conversation.
Now you are gone.

Whenever I get back to New York I keep looking
for all the droll beauties you mention,
the mere and the great,
including the possibilities of Khrushchev,
hoping, the same as you,
the day is the right day.

On a Remark by the Poet,
Dana Gioia, on Translating

Translation is inevitable, in the first place,
because of the curse of Babel ...

Robert M. Adams

It is sheer coveting, that much is clear,
of someone else's folly and surprise,
and soothes your secret fever as you peer
into another person's heart, to see
with calm, untroubled eyes,
how things may be and how things may not be.
The act of a voyeur,
you spy a fellow out, and take his lies
for granted, your own motives less than pure.
Then you fix his measure, take a look
in a strange dictionary, and try your luck.

Out of the poem you gingerly extract
the live-coal from the clinker in the grate;
then envy glosses into cunning tact,
the shimmering in your hands. By fits and starts
you ponder, study, weigh, you extricate
from gritty clots the gleaming private parts.
Soon it's like keeping score;
your pencil flails away, moods don't distract,
and the grisly business leaves no trace of gore.
When you are finished, watch him strut and rage;
it isn't you that's crying in the cage.

This will not do for Homer, you've been told,
or Dante. Shakespeare has the best of it
for changing englished Plutarch into gold.
That wasn't alchemy, but outright theft.
No doubt our mother wit
does well enough—though we are all bereft
since Babel's shame—
to strike a phrase cast from our own stronghold,
but you're translating now, so stake your claim—
we're babbling foreigners all, and none the worse
for Bibles put to native prose and verse.

At the Widow Kate's Retirement Banquet

The guest of honor sits, as patient as
the furniture, and listens maybe to our talk
about her service to the cold country
of working for a living forty years,
and raising up three kids without a man.
Among the cataracts of drapes, the cliffs of glass,
she gleams, the slender willow by the stream
of our smooth conversation, the fragile fact.
And old boys joke, and the Big Boss swoops down
from the eagle's nest of his democracy
to grasp her by the hand, and wish her well;
while all she does, like a willow by a stream
in sunlight, is to toss her flowing hair.

Spoiled by All My Tyrants

Spoiled by all my tyrants, and whomped to bed,
but kissed for my blond curls from time to time,
then shoved to school like the bound refugee
Authority had asked for, all my brothers
gruff and soon gone growing, to come back
and bring me all the grace of the Green Fair,
I had a precious training, and clean hands.
On the cold bench my mother creaked her grief
to understand my words; the school salute
I pressed upon the flag could only scare her.
O my dark kind, why have you left me bleating,
to learn trite courtesies and lowland ways,
when all I wanted was my rightful place
as the last son beside my father's table?
Tell him that as I grow my hair turns darker.

The Marionettes

See how they dream their wooden dreams,
pine legends in their painted eyes.
Their ardor is of crepe and chalk;
the fire is their only surprise.

Catch how they mouth their gargoyle talk;
they even love with a scratching sound.
The fire is their only surprise,
Pinocchio burning himself to the ground.

Watch how they dance their clacking dance;
their kiss is like the breaking of a box.
They would sprout leaves, like fingers of sense—
Master Gepetto, how they dance,

sauntering past with chirping knees
through the proscenium's feast of eyes.
Wanting not to made of wood,
the fire is their only surprise.

City of iron metaphors,
your children applaud their angular pranks
as their freak noses bump in fiction.
Do they hope that mothers will offer thanks?

See how they turn their necks of bark,
wound and wired for noise and friction.

They are not children lost in the dark.
The fire is their only surprise.

Friend Cricket, like a piccolo,
you weep from the wall of your prophecy:
they are so lonely racked on the shelves;
they can weep splinters if only they try.

They're not content to be themselves,
but plot a vegetable sovereignty,
with their sinister, sonorous Italian names
dreaming some varnished mythology.

The fire is their only surprise.
They court the green and yellow courtesan;
in her silver dress she is telling them lies.
The moon is their favorite citizen.

And all unsteadied by their pilgrimage
to this last boondock of a grimy town.
visited by their pushcart prompt parades
I spy a hundred wooden strangers in the lemon dawn.

They are shouting I love you in an old dialect,
their chatterbox tarantellas waking the glades—
Columbina, the barking of Melampo,
the toy apples of Giuseppina's breasts,

shimmering forth from the ultimate shores of illusion,
Puncinello, staring with eyes of pearl,
singing I love the child with the blue hair,
I love the green and yellow girl.

II.

The Bocce Court on Lewis Avenue

The Bocce Court on Lewis Avenue

The poem that follows is, I guess, a praise-song for the old neighborhood where I grew up. I think poetry started as praise and supplication, and celebrated triumphs, defeats, weddings, and Deity. I believe all poets, at some time or other in their creative lives, feel a strong nostalgia for the legendary beginnings of their craft, and, I have to own up to it here, I have yielded to the engrossing temptations of such feelings, and tried to be a bard. For those readers who would like to ponder this concept further, I can offer no better suggestion than an engagement with Mary Renault's biographical novel, *The Praise Singer,* where she imagines with flair and scholarship the life of Simonides, (6th century B. C.), an ancient poet who followed Homer.

Corona, scene of the action of my poem, was in my childhood an old, neat, dowdy, peaceful section of Queens, a borough of New York City which used to be called in those days "the borough of small homes." (Its main claim to fame today is as the home of the New York Mets baseball team, Shea Stadium.) To give one an incisive idea of the stakes involved in the "war" between Mayor Lindsay (1970) and Corona Heights, one need only reflect chastely that $45,000 homes were being condemned by New York City at a surrender price of $21,000.

The struggle of these few people over a no longer unimportant tract of land bounded by a dump, vast car junk-yards, and the busy IRT subway system, attracted national attention—much joking by TV reporters especially—and vociferous support of celebrities such as Norman Mailer and Jimmy Breslin. The four-year war was a heroic story, and deserves a poem.

I close with an excerpt from the *New York Times* that describes, in cold detail, the capitulation of the Mighty to the wrath of the people:

From a *New York Times* story, December 3, 1970—

New Corona Plan
Spares 59 Homes

City to return 31, move 28
in Compromise on School

Fifty-one homeowners in Corona,
Queens, who had fought vainly for
three years against displacement for a
proposed high school, won an extra-
ordinary last-minute reprieve yester-
day at City Hall.

The city, which already had taken
title to their homes in a fight most
people thought was over, offered to
return the property of 31 owners and
to move the small frame and cinder-
block houses of 28 others to new sites
a block away.

The compromise was described as
the first time in which the city had
ever offered to return a large tract of
property taken in eminent domain. . . .

The Bocce Court on Lewis Avenue

—New York Times photograph, December 2, 1970, by Barton Silverman

1. The center of the shot

That man caught in the center of the shot—
right arm thrust forward, shoulder jutting out—
is shooting, has released his bocce ball
with line-drive fury, cunning underhand
at his opponent's ball close to the ball—
the tiny one—that gives the winning point.
The trick is to put spin into his throw
so that the flung ball arcs into its target
and grinds on contact with the enemy
and knocks it clean away, yet stays in place
itself, snug-dug into the dirt. You call that english,
which is pool-player's jargon good enough
for any old Italian playing bocce.
The ball is coming at you with great speed.
A good displacement makes a popping sound
of wood on wood, like a revolver-shot,
and this is what the word *sparata* means,
the word spectators cry if the ball hits.
Displacement is the dearest thing in bocce;
not dump-shot, not home run, it can reverse a point,
turn losers into winners. This leads to drinking.
Here, as displacement, it is kinder than
the one the mayor plans, our suave John Lindsay,
who has ordered the demolition of this street,
this bocce court four generations old,
to make room for a high school playing-field.

2. *The left border of the photograph*

Look at the beefy man in the business suit
loitering at the edge of the photograph
behind the low plank fence that frames the court.
He's a little shifty. He has no business there.
He should be on the job. He stole away
more like a burglar than the banking man
he is in real life. He's the mortgage-man
at the Corona Savings Bank, the one
these bocce players save at, up the block.
He's glancing at his wrist watch, but that's sham,
and not his conscience; he has time enough.
His paperwork is all tied up—no deals;
the whole town is agog with condemnation,
the talk of lawyers' notices, and rumor
is running through the streets like a cold wind.
But what the hell, he thinks, time on his hands;
the game's a hot one: he'll just bum a drink,
and maybe place a bet.

              The jug of wine is set
beneath the bench those men are sitting on
at the court's far end. They face the camera,
they watch the game, conversing in low tones.
In front of them, of course, and in the way,
the mailman stands—note the insignia

on his left shoulder— weaving from side to side
and tilting over in anxiety
because the ball just thrown is headed for
his point-ball. He's the opponent of the man
who flung the ball straight at the camera.
He's almost dancing now, and doubled over,
wishing up a jinx of pure distraction;
you'd think that he was dodging someone's aim—
he is; he doesn't want to be displaced.
His fists are clenched; the frown upon his face
is fierce enough to scare the little boy
whom you can't see, behind the privet hedge
that forms the border of the photograph.
The boy is squatting, hiding from the man
who threw the ball, his father. He'd been told
at least five minutes past to scoot back home
and pick up some cigars. The innocent fact
is that he cannot tear himself away.
He is afraid that if he goes away
his father, his strong father, will not win.
He too is wishing up a mighty jinx,
his fingers crossed against the tilting mailman.
Of course the whole town's wishing up a jinx
to topple City Hall, and save the homes.

3. The right border of the photograph

The ball's still in the air. This poem has wings.
Those three men to the right of your frozen stare,
almost outside the frame, each with one foot
perched on the sacrosanct old plank
that separates them from the bocce game
(they look as though they want to jump inside)
are the Greek chorus here. They may not know that.
They're young, and off from work, or between jobs.
You stand around a lot in Corona Heights:
it's easy—there's the coffee shop, the park,
an ice cream parlor with Italian ices,
and Leo's Pizzeria. There's this game.
One fellow, eyes intent upon the ball,
is muttering out of one side of his mouth
to the fellow next to him. You hear it all.
"We should all go on strike, my mother said.
I said to her, Ma! Go on strike, what strike?
How can I go on strike if I ain't working?"
The others laugh. Now the three shift
in unison, as to cue, from turn
to counter-turn; they're following the ball.
They murmur; things are coming up Act Five.
At that same moment the small cameraman
inside your head is wondering to himself
if this will be the shot that gets the page.

In this seedy part of Queens, where no one goes
unless it's home, the machinery is in place
to bring the ball down, like a god, with wings.

4. Foreground

Yes, you are hearing something; that's a voice
you hear. Those women chattering aren't in the picture,
but have just met a few feet from the court
on the cracked sidewalk. Now they stop to talk
about the story in the *Daily News,*
the one describing once again their anger,
the tactics they have used to show resistance
to progress, as the politicians call it—
the worry for their homes, the neighborhood,
their frugal habits, simple histories,
and the surprising sensible suggestion
that Jimmy Breslin offered, in a column,
that maybe all the old homes could be moved,
and not demolished. It is a last hope.
The middle-aged woman, celery sticking out
of her shopping bag, an inch below her nose,
is fuming. As she shakes her head the greens
tremble their little flags, and her voice rises:
"The lawyer from the City said to me
that we could put my mother in a home
after we left. He could arrange for it.

I said to him, I said, I'll scrub floors first.
That's not the way we treat our people here."
The younger woman swings her handbag up
to point a finger at the cameraman:
another foot and she could smack him square
in the head with it. "I told that man to come
and see my fig tree, take a picture maybe.
The one my father planted. I told him,
these are my memories, this house, that tree.
How do you pay for memories, I said."

5. *The frame to hold the photograph*

Behind the scene the mayor's playing ball—
that bocce ball's his stone of Sisyphus—
with the local politicians just as quick
if not as slick as he is, not as pretty.
The struggle of the homes is out of hand:
old women and children chanting, homemade posters
nailed to the telephone poles, the TV clip
of a moustachioed codger standing by
a bulldozer and aiming his old shotgun.
The gaggle of reporters is shocked and pleased
to find their startling feature a few blocks
from the IRT, in rowdy-dowdy Queens.
The Mayor contemplates a walking tour
of Lewis Avenue in his shirt sleeves

46

the way he did in Harlem, where it worked.
No, Cary Grant, you'll shed more than a crease
if you do that, and meet up with these people.
They'll greet you with their ancient imprecations,
oaths of ancestors, feats of profanity
admired even by some poets and scholars,
like, say, Henri Michaux, who in hushed lines
once spoke in awe of "Neapolitan calumny,"
the kind to make a man drop dead in shame.
Your mayoral campaign has hit the skids;
one thing seems sure—you'll not be re-elected.
The Boards of Estimate, of City Planning,
of Education, a huge over-world
of bureaucrats and condemnation lawyers
(like Cuomo), precinct captains, the gauleiters
of the two major parties have sniffed the wind
of national as well as local rumor.
To use the old cliché, they are all laughing stock
for both comedians and columnists.
Laughter is not their business; money is;
this is a gang that has to save its ass.

Read, in snatches, their statement to the press—
. . . . *deplores the tactics.* . . . *three and a half years.* . . .
of hardship for the 69 families. . . .
must not occur again. . . . *delay and anguish.* . . .
deputy mayor (Lindsay will not be quoted)
denies duplicity. . . . Corona Heights

is maimed, but saved, some houses moved, five demolished.
The Battle of Bad Acres has been won
by a few angry people, and a fig tree.

6. Blast of music

At Leo's Pizzeria *Vo-Lah-re*'s playing
on the machine that lights up like a steamboat.
The guys and gals are watching the TV
that's turned down low, Gabe Pressman on the screen.
One fellow, coming out of the Men's Room,
bursts into tremolo, *nel blu dipinto di blu* . . .
as the bartender, telling him to shut up,
darts out to the nickelodeon, pulls the cord,
stands splay-footed, eyes riveted to the screen.
Suddenly Gabe Pressman fills the place;
his soothing voice drifts over the dark room,
almost a homily, and gives the news,
the statement. Names are named. They lift wolf cries,
pound the bar and punch up on each other,
grins on their faces. Now the bartender
re-plugs the nickelodeon, and darts back
to hustle drinks, and when the music blares
they sing along. Gabe Pressman stares and stares.

7. *Center*

Back at the bocce court the photograph
is hatching in the black and silver box.
Tomorrow, like a swooping bird, the ball
the old man flung will spread across the pages
of the *New York Times,* and all the other papers.
The little boy who disobeyed his father
is standing now. Squatting was no fun.
His eyes are wide and darting; he wrings his hands
an instant, and then gives a hesitant clap,
quivering as he tries to skip and jump,
yet not be noticed. Now his blushing face
is the round O his lips make crying out.
He feels his heart careening, plunging down
with the plunging ball. Ah, that colliding crack
of wood on wood as loud as demolition,
sparata: the shot heard round City Hall.
He whirls into a dance, then checks himself.
The way he races home now you would think
he thinks he bears a message from the gods.
Behind him a voice shouts, "It's on the News . . ."
He takes it for the wind that speeds him on.

III.

Geographies

. . . not the object described, but the light that falls on it,
like the lamp from a distant room.

Boris Pasternak

The Old Clothes Tree

leans in the hall
and wobbles now and then
beneath his pack.
Not what he used to be.

But last night I dreamed
he swirled his cape of laundry
twirled his bent umbrella
dancing in the dark.

This morning
rushing past
I brushed against him.
He flailed his empty sleeves
in a little jig
and tossed his hat
in the air.

Midwest Fantasy

1. Winter: Red's Barbershop

Boys who played the games they've always played,
at nine years old, at forty nine years old,
the snow, the moose, the lake, the air so cold
it hurt to breathe, as someone said,
calling to his buddies up ahead—
he slipped into an icy ditch, and spilled
his guts caroming, but his rib-cage held.
He laughed and laughed. His buddies called him mad.

The barbershop is buzzing up a storm
of memories this snow-sharp afternoon, some boys
as full of liquor as they are of noise,
such is the fellowship that keeps them warm.
Later, back home, their women will cut loose
at them about that moose, that bloody stupid moose.

2. Spring: The Mourning Dove

The mourning dove, soft idiot on my sill,
pecks at the glass. Surprised it does not yield
he straightens up, and blinks his button eye,
and like a small parade struts back and forth,
then shows his white behind and flies away.

3. Summer: August

This heavy hour,
this ton of light;
the blinding pane,
all I can do is squint

at the garden with its look
of frost in early dawn,
where a cricket is making music.
The mirage cuts like a knife.

Then I stare as hard as I can
at the squirrel in the pawpaw branch
not three feet from the window.
He is heaving, heaving.

I think of the flameshapes of the corn,
tumescent and gold,
that point and point.
Where my dream walks they cackle.

4. Autumn: Indiana

Now the sheaves crackle
to the touch, like new dollar bills.
Glowing October. The irrigation pond
shimmers.

Like a stampede the stand of trees
in the distance shudders its green mane—
glint and ripple of shadow,
mist on the ground running silver.

The ditch by the road heaves with plumes.
A rock shows its head among the yarrow.
Poetry is a gun
aimed at the fat hare trundling across

the field. He comes to a stop,
sits up, ears twitching.
I have been at my window all morning,
my page covered with the showering thresher's dust
that flirts in the breeze like gauze,
like a flag.

The Hunters

The hunters from the city, strictly dressed
in store-bought reds and yellows, trailing smells
of shaving lotion, board the country train.
With pale and jolly looks they settle down
in the far corner, weapons clattering
in small, efficient shocks, start playing cards
slapped on an old valise across their knees.
They've come to rent our poor and shaggy county;
they sprawl in corduroy poses, noisily,
while lower on the skyline, the sun setting
chips over river into scales and whorls
that float downstream, like scattered, golden feathers.

On Painting a Bike

The weather, like a tourist here before,
returns in patch and plaid to lawn and tree;
three robins repossess the courteous shore
of our brick lake, and scold the continent.
The children's bicycles are blue this year;
I wonder now what last year's colors meant.

In my own childhood, when the weather came,
April or May, I felt a busy need
to be at painting—it was like a game
of changing all the furniture of the earth,
made up of bikes and wagons it would seem;
I brushed away for all that I was worth.

I took such satisfaction in my stain
I caused the garden in the back to glow,
and those old irons glimmered in the rain
like famous weapons fabulous to win.
Mine was a landscape painted over then
might make a proper serpent change his skin.

Now I'm turning gray; the season's green;
there's not a single fault that I can dye.
Some kids ride past, each eager to be seen,
with arms outspread, like wings, as after all
I did myself once, till I had a spill
that skinned me red as Eden in the fall.

From an Apartment House Window

Outside, the cars sleep peacefully, like sheep
huddled in asphalt valleys. Over all,
the moon, imagined shepherd, seems to creep
by yard and building, and by sagging wall,
a quiet figure in a field of brick.
There is a stillness here would surely suit
Theocritus, more than my rhetoric
that dreams these stones would ring to hear his flute.

Binary Rhymes

What are the generations of the fly?
The logarithms of astronomy

can measure them in all their magnitude,
compute the leaves that populate a wood.

Numbers, numbers, are the current rage.
Are the sands beyond number beyond reach?

With metaphysical machines that count
piano-rolls of algebraic cant

we manufacture meanings where there was
mere wordless music, dunes, shaggy grass.

O lovely lotteries, o chips and chance!
It is for principle I stay a dunce.

Irises

Time's lackey, but the lord of sun this day,
I watch the garden from my window, glance
at the green rubble rusting in the clay
of my new-city suburb, note the pert
irises at their posture by the fence,
resembling cardboard figures stuck in dirt.

Concordance and construction in their sure
trim rods, from which the leaves, like blades,
work on the wind the menace of their humor,
I marvel that their flags now fly so limp.
In all the brick and hazard of these shades
the sun had lent his legendary lamp

and shone, a Hero, who was not. They stand,
plumage awry now, swords askew, like troops
at ease in a parade from Bogus Land
where generals led the armies down wrong streets;
they crack in wind like locusts, like all hopes
faltered in alternating hails and heats.

Where is my sin of cynicism here?
I am no long fellow, with words of worth,
to argue celebration at a bier,
when, for a week perhaps, they get their wish
before they tumble once again to earth,
the blonde and tousled head, the ragged flesh.

The Insect World

Poised paradox, whose slender, clever claws
Resemble, maybe, hands that clasp in prayer,
Artfully scythed to sweep a struggling spouse
Young to your breast, while his legs thrash the air
In frantic waltz, his flesh your wedding feast,
Nomenclature's humor suits you least.
Grass widow, yours is grief I do not share.

Monsters of childhood glimmer from your face,
Amaze the singing meadow. Robots stalk
Near rose and garden hedge, by Queen Anne's lace,
Tumbling the simple buggers for a lunch.
Insect, or pious preacher, little hawk,
Serving up sermons, all you say is Crunch.

The Motel at the End of the Ramp

Our hamburgers ooze like the blob
from outer space. We are all tired
and trivial. We are eager pioneers
believing that whatever it is we do
it is best to get there in a tremendous hurry—
buns through a car window, and the plastic cups
rolling in the wind on the asphalt
of the American dream. We are young;
we are old and overfed, in Hawaiian shirts.
Our children are smeared with ketchup like blood.
Here then, Thomas Jefferson, is your miracle.

Our roads all lead to roam another horizon,
suburbs attached to them like barnacles;
in the dangerous wash of our wealth
the hills soar and dive like sounding whales.
Why poetry? what glamors here is the motel
at the end of the ramp, lit up like the Titanic,
before the great iceberg of history.
People are zooming in, and zooming out,
young couples, families, the well-dressed terrorists.
I doze to good old Mancini on the Muzak;
I sleep to a whine of trucks, and god-loud thunder.

Andrew

Friend, heavy survivor,
you bear the bull's lowered brow,
ready for comers.

To look at you is to understand
jungles are not nice.
My mind creates tableaux

set behind glass—don't touch—
in memory's museum,
especially one of a classroom

and teacher calling you wop.
Or that night in Linden Park
when, head lowered,

you told me your mother was dead.
We were fourteen,
completely uncomforted.

I suppose things are better today.
We are offered courses on dying.
The joggers tell us, Love yourself.

Old puff-belly baldhead,
you listen to your kids complain,
and smile.

You make a killing at the track
and zoom home in your huge car,
full of frowns.

For you a proverb might be set:
do not thank the gods too loudly,
or they will hear you and change their minds.

Brother, fellow loser,
I know why in these enlightened times
you still tend the Sacred Heart

on the wall
outside your bedroom
with fragrant candles:

it is the one trophy you understand,
as Jesus taught—
we are all nailed to the wall.

The Metaphysics of Winter

Here is a stone whose rugged round
on this November afternoon
glows from the center of its mound
of leaves, and looks just like the moon.
It is not smooth, but hard and bright,
as what will happen pretty soon,
when the green garden changes light
and what shines bright will shine like bone.
Then sun and moon, pure incident,
like Cain and Abel where they went
will daze and dazzle earth turned stone,
like the first skull of Testament.

Two Translations

UMBERTO SABA: *Ulysses*

When I was young I sailed the Dalmatian coast.
Great islands bloomed on the wave; above them flew
once in a while a bird in search of prey.
Covered with kelp, and slippery, under the sun
they shone as beautiful as emeralds.
When night came, and in the high tide they vanished,
with our sails underwind we ducked for the deep
to flee that perilous snare. Today, like that,
my kingdom is No Man's Land. My harbor
burns lanterns for foreigners, and I turn back to sea,
pressed ever on by my unbeaten spirit,
and by my broken-hearted love of life.

UMBERTO SABA: *The Boy and the Shrike*

A boy became enamored of a shrike.
It was a novelty of what he heard
a hunter say about that marvellous bird:
How many vows he made to own a shrike!

He got one, and forgot her, just like that.
Poor bird, strung up inside her window-cage,
she mourned alone in silence for the sky
far off, and irretrievable to her sight.

He only thought of her a certain day
when, out of boredom, or some kind of spite,
he clenched her in his fist, and felt a pain.
She bit him, and flew off. And since that day,

and for that hurt, he loves her all in vain.

Elegy, 1942

Fort Devens, Massachusetts

Dowd was the old man of the company,
the one we listened to. He taught us tricks,
like sewing, or he showed us how to roll
a cigarette, or how to take stove black
and cover over cracks in a worn locker
and make it shine. Whenever he got drunk
he'd sing, in a low whisper, some old tune,
"An Orphan and in love," and go to sleep.
He cowed those blackjack players in the back
who liked to stay up late, and swear and smoke,
and keep us all awake, night after night.
When Dowd was by, we slept like innocents.

He heard Cerruti swearing once, and ribbed him,
told him that was some prayer the seminary
was teaching all the boys. Cerruti blinked,
and kept on blinking, searching for the words.
"That seminary is none of your business."
We all knew that Cerruti had washed out
of the seminary, and gone home. In shame
he left home then—imagine—for the Army.
Big Dowd leaned over him, grinned, shook his head:
"It's guys like me who swear. We don't know words.
That leaves holes in the head we paper over
with swear-words. You have learning. You should read,
and study things, not try to be like us."
He walked away. Cerruti blinked again,
and lowered his head to buff his combat boots.

Dowd was shipped out. It was for convoy duty,
an anti-aircraft crew. His empty cot
was taken over soon by someone else,
and that was that. We all forgot about him
except Cerruti; they kept in touch with cards,
and then the cards stopped coming. Came a day,
months later, Nally told us Dowd got his
in the North Sea. The whole convoy went down.

Cerruti dropped his boots, and walked outside;
I watched him through the window, pacing, blinking,
kicking at gravel, searching for the words,
until like death-besotted Lear he shouted
fuck it fuck it fuck it fuck it fuck it.

Hubie

Army experiments with mixed units:
Negroes being admitted into white
companies.—

News Item, 1943

You, Hubie, were the one and only black
in our whole crazy outfit. You had a knack
for fending off our clumsy comradeship.
You were a ferret at a Freudian slip
or condescension: (Let's ask Hubie, too!)
You always answered, "Cut it out, will you?"
Except one time: the night we made to go
to the Anselmo Club, and wouldn't you know,
we challenged you, we forced you, kidnapped you
to come along. You came. We wrecked the place.
The frightened 4F doorman mentioned race,
held his hand up to his pasty face,
and said you had no card, no "membership,"
He tried to close the door; Paul knocked his grip,
and hollered, "He's our guest!" Then the poor guy said No,
and Paul, half drunk already, just let go.
That was a fight we all enjoyed but you;
the cops came, and your black skin saved our hides,
because the owner blamelessly denied
that there was trouble, and we made no news.
No news was good for him, and good for us,
but the drink you drank that night was bitter, bitter juice.

Then there was Captain Jones from Millidgeville
(GEE-AY!) who hated you so hard it killed

to hear him give you his Boy-this, Boy-that.
He hated all of us, but that was pure so what
to the dockside bruisers, city toughs,
and all the ill-sorted country roughs
that made up our sad clan of prison-chasers:
we knew that you were the true King of Losers.
Maybe that's why we liked you, let that stay,
from ignorance to shame to light of day.
Jones ran us like a chain-gang, that's for sure,
but your bland moon-face shone, "Endure, endure."

Once I glimpsed you with the Enemies.
It was their singing time. They were a breeze
to guard, no trouble. It was a heavy night
of stars and blooms, of shadows that turned bright.
A kid cupped his right hand up to his face
the way they did to magnify the voice,
and winked at you. Hubie, you winked back.
It was a sign between you for a song,
and then he gave their yodel, loud and long,
fronni e limoni; which maybe signified
some legend lost when ancient glory died,
but left its echo. No one would begin
before the signal, *lemon leaves,* had run
in gross annunciation. The same phrase
would introduce each stanza. In a daze
I heard the eerie music, though this time

the voice I heard was yours, in Neapolitan rhyme,
and my translation of it here is a crime:

Oh leaves of the lemon trees! It's in the shape of crosses
they are constructed, all the gates of prison,
the better to destroy the sons of mothers.
Ah, Hubie, what a maundering in my heart
to hear you go falsetto, sob and start,
and grace-note that muezzin-vaunt of words,
gliding the vowels over, like slow birds,
the drawn out line. I thought my head would burst.
For their lament those lads made you sing first;
you knew the chant; it could have been the blues,
three lines of heartbreak, blood down to your shoes.
Then came the answers, in the same old notes,
one fellow, then another, golden throats—
tears for a mother, or a girl back home,
some nasty verse on the Pope in Rome,
and when your turn came round again you sang
about the way the bells of Nola rang.
Mad Captain Jones's "damn eye-talian crew"
had caught your grave compassion, trusted you,
and taught you more Italian for a song
than the rest of us had learned the whole year long.
Those distant bells, they did you no more good,
than did the chimes of elegant Englewood,
New Jersey, where you came from, preacher's son,
out of a tiny Baptist congregation

made up of cooks and gardeners, garbage men,
and other service people all hemmed in.
The war came, you were ready, just like me,
which meant no job, no future, and no money.

What now comes back to me, old Hubie, is
how you and I could sit and shoot the breeze
those Sunday afternoons, when things went dead
in repple-depple camp. The peace went to my head.
We chuckled about week-end roll-calls, played
the same each muster: mostly, no one up
except us cowards who were thin on hope,
afraid to miss the check and rate KP,
although in truth half our company
slept through. The guys took turns as stand-ins, one
for every two or three in mock attention,
answering for O'Toole or Policetti
or Garbatino. Sergeant Parmelee
stared straight down at his pad, and called the lot,
then swung around to go back to his cot.
"Why don't you slack off, Hubie?" I asked once.
You snorted, as though you took me for a dunce,
patted my knee with that ham hand of yours,
and said, "Because for me it would just be my arse.
With my complexion can't you see the fun?"
The simple truth fell on me like a ton.

Poor twins, we were discharged on the same day,
a lot to do, pick up our pay,
strip down our cots—"They might just change their minds,"
our sergeant snarled, "so move your fat behinds"—
sweep out the years, go listen to the lecture
on Re-enlistment and Reserve, some double feature;
then scoot to chow, and back to Camp Supply.

The Quartermaster goof-off, Sleepy Eye,
just brushed our gear aside, and made us sign.
On our way out we passed a clothing bin;
talk about brave! I knew we were civilians
when I snitched a cap, an Eisenhower jacket,
and so did you, you bum, and you said, "Fuck it!"
The whole platoon was gone when we got back,
the silence of the barracks pure whip-crack
of memories in my head. I stared at you.
You said, "There's still one thing for us to do,"
and handed me a sheet, hodge-podge
of name, address, and Bible verse for pledge
all loyalty, no betrayal. To make things worse
I read aloud that thundering, crying verse,
because you told me once I was a poet.
What boobs we were; how kind we didn't know it.
I handed you a map of streets, instructions,
accompanied by four-letter imprecations
of what would happen if you didn't write me,

or come and visit. Then you'd have to fight me.
The map showed names of streets and bus route numbers.
All at once we stopped. We were struck dumb.
You blinked your eyes, and made a choking noise.
That was enough for me; I lost my voice.

We neither of us wrote. What came
between? It was not a forgetting. It was time
that took its aim, and brought us down like fools.
We had survived—according to the rules—
the deaths, the separations, all the cant
of war, of honor, and the special rant
of patriotism. We had saved our skins
through years of soldiering, the tightrope dance
of danger, boredom, whatever we fought for;
ourselves, we knew, were the true spoils of war.
We moved from that into the orgy of
the personal release of pure self-love.

The time is gone for what we should have said
or done, old Hubie. All the dead are dead.
Time was once ripe. Now time's a rotten thought.
Yet blow me down, and scratch me for an ought,
we buddied to the end, just to endure.
(There is a thought here that is less than pure.)

A black man and a white man, that's for sure,
this other war, and the cagey cowardice

of habit, turning honest blood to ice.
I think that we were brothers once, "The Twins,"
the fellows called us, masking their wide grins.
What's left is poetry, the penance for my sins.

Honorable Army Discharge

My heart was full of money, and my head
was full of dreams, the day that I got home
for good. My mother cried and cried, my sisters
cried; my brother, turned fourteen, just stared
and laughed, and stuck his finger to his head
and rolled his eyes. It was as if to say
that things were back to normal now, and crazy.

When Pop came home from work, harroomph, harroomph,
he asked me if I'd been to see my room,
the new paint job. He tripped upon a word,
said something about a new bloom sweeping clean.

That broke things up, we laughed, we all sat down
to eat and talk. I choked the pasta down
as best I could; it was so rich and sweet,
the taste of a largesse I had forgotten.
I never guessed at yearning, those lost years,
until late in the night. The new paint job
seared through my nostrils, and brought out the tears,
my room so small, so safe, so quiet I heard
the drumming in my ears, my heart's own cannon
time and again go whoosh and whoosh and thud.

The Veteran

Four hundred poems ago
my time off was a conspiracy
to undermine the Muse's citadel;
I worked bombs at my desk.

Now, thoughts of winding down by noon-time,
my beer like a bubble bath . . .

thoughts of the sunny garden,
that new book on ancient Greece,
and our tilted sundial casting its shadow
towards the grackles, who don't care.

Unbudgeable, and full of light,
the hollow hackberry stump by the fence
grins like a mouth;
there are vines at the base trailing upward.
For a moment I recall
the trappings of Dionysus,
the god in the tree.

Nobody has to tell me
poems are of the earth,
craft trains the vine.

For that reason I keep worry away
in a doze, in a dream

of Apollonian summer,
my torch doused in the sun.

In a city as out of date
as Edna St. Vincent Millay
a young poet once burned his candle at both ends,
and starved himself for a book.

Look at him now, smiling,
paunch-happy
like that old Tabby, no leopard cub,
sniffing at the tree stump
before him.
The poet's wife, no maenad,
brings him another beer.
Fame be damned.